Out-of-Sight
PHOTO PUZZLES

Adam Ritchey

PUZZLE
WRIGHT
PRESS

An imprint of Sterling
Publishing Co., Inc.
www.puzzlewright.com

For Jackson

Puzzlewright Press and the distinctive Puzzlewright Press logo
are registered trademarks of Sterling Publishing Co., Inc.

2   4   6   8   10   9   7   5   3

Published by Sterling Publishing Co., Inc.
387 Park Avenue South, New York, NY 10016
© 2010 by Adam Ritchey
Distributed in Canada by Sterling Publishing
c/o Canadian Manda Group, 165 Dufferin Street
Toronto, Ontario, Canada M6K 3H6
Distributed in the United Kingdom by GMC Distribution Services
Castle Place, 166 High Street, Lewes, East Sussex, England BN7 1XU
Distributed in Australia by Capricorn Link (Australia) Pty. Ltd.
P.O. Box 704, Windsor, NSW 2756, Australia

Sterling ISBN 978-1-4027-7080-7

For information about custom editions, special sales, premium and
corporate purchases, please contact Sterling Special Sales
Department at 800-805-5489 or specialsales@sterlingpublishing.com.

Contents

Introduction 5

Puzzles

    Easy 6

    Medium 42

    Hard 78

    Killer 110

Answers 130

Introduction

Welcome to *Out-of-Sight Photo Puzzles*! You'll need to observe the obscure, spot the subtle, and dig up the details to solve these decidedly dizzying puzzles. While you're at it, you'll visit county fairs and ski trails, rub shoulders with bicyclists and beachgoers, and hobnob with penguins and dolphins.

This book features six different types of picture puzzles. Here's how they work:

Spot the Differences 1

In this classic puzzle, you are challenged to find the differences between two seemingly identical photographs. Some of the changes are obvious while others are subtle. For each puzzle we've noted how many changes you can find.

Spot the Differences 2

Like the other type of Spot the Differences puzzle, here you'll again be looking for changes made in photographs. Except in this version, you are challenged to find only one difference each between the top photo and the four photos below. Each photo has a single, different modification than the others do.

Identical Images

These puzzles have one simple rule: Just find the two images that are completely identical. Or to think of it another way, it's "Spot the Lack of Differences"!

Hidden Objects

Using the small sample image given, find the multiple identical objects hidden somewhere in the large photo. They may be partially obscured behind other objects in the scene.

Missing Pieces

In this puzzle, we've taken one big photograph and pulled out twelve small squares from it. All you need to do is figure out where they belong! Use the grid coordinates as your guide. But, be warned: in the Hard and Killer levels, we've taken the additional step of rotating the squares. Some are rotated left, some are rotated right, and some are turned upside down.

Mixed-Up Images

And for the final puzzle type included in the book, three different (but related) photographs have been chopped into quarters, and then mixed up. Your challenge is to discern the details that will allow you to put the images back together again.

That's all you need to know! To get started, just turn the page. And don't worry about making any faux pas. In this book, it's polite to stare!

—Adam Ritchey

Fair Play

Hut One! Hut Two!

What's Up, Dock?

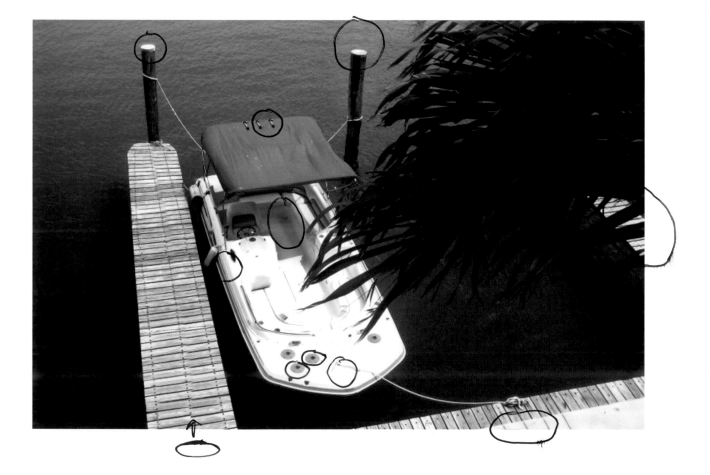

Hello, Yellow

Can you locate the small images below in the large picture?

Answer on page 131

1: B13   7: F13
2: G4   8: A2
3: D8   9: F2
4: A12   10: B5
5: D4   11: E10
6: H3   12: B10

Hi, Hyacinth

Can you locate the small images below in the large picture?

Answer on page 131

1: _____   7: _____

2: _____   8: _____

3: _____   9: _____

4. _____   10: _____

5: _____   11: _____

6: _____   12: _____

Vine and Dandy

Each image has exactly one difference with the top photo. Can you find them all? Answer on page 131

❶

❷

❸

❹

Columns As You See 'Em

Each image has exactly one difference with the top photo. Can you find them all? Answer on page 131

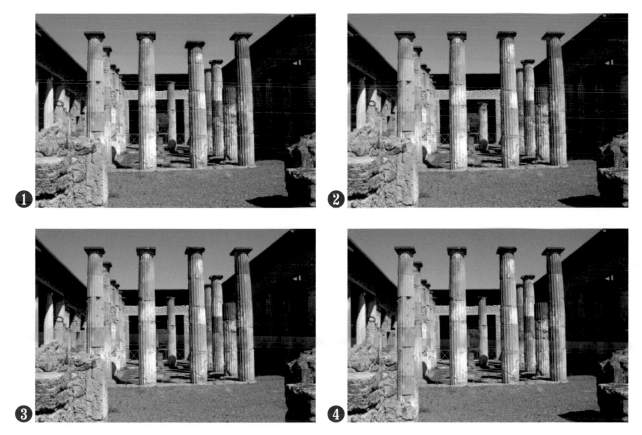

A Horse, of Course

Home on the Orange

12
differences

Answers
on page 132

Keep score:

Orange on the Home

Can you find the ten oranges hidden in the photo below?

Answer on page 132

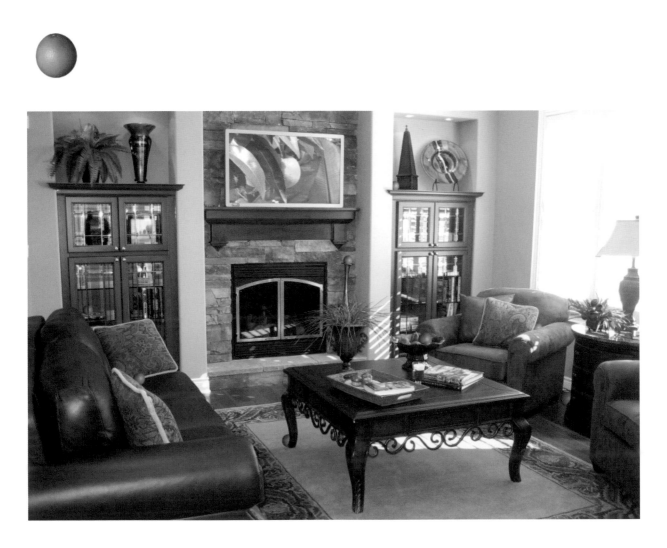

Tennis, Anywhere?

Can you find the seven tennis balls hidden in the photo below?

Answer on page 132

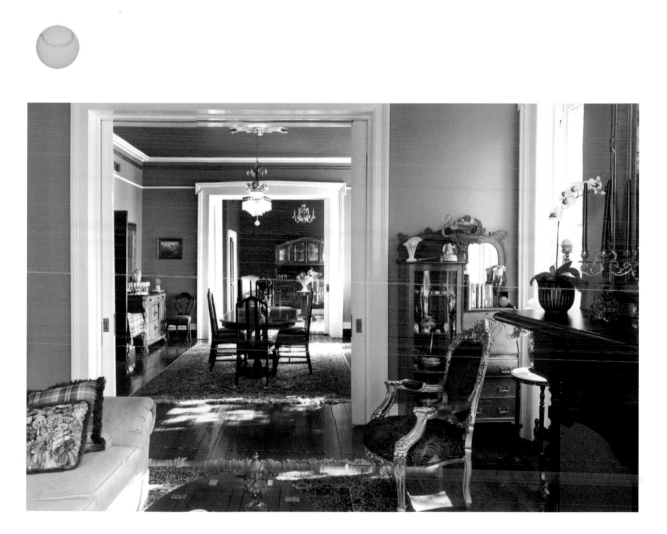

Bumper Stumper

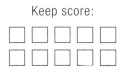

10
differences

Answers
on page 132

Keep score:

☐ ☐ ☐ ☐ ☐
☐ ☐ ☐ ☐ ☐

Making a Splash

Which two of these photos are exactly alike?

Answer on page 132

Taking a Leap

Which two of these photos are exactly alike?

Answer on page 133

① ② ③ ④ ⑤ ⑥

Tunnel Vision

10
differences

Answers
on page 133

Keep score:

☐ ☐ ☐ ☐ ☐
☐ ☐ ☐ ☐ ☐

Texas Two-Step

10 differences

Answers on page 133

Keep score:

☐ ☐ ☐ ☐ ☐
☐ ☐ ☐ ☐ ☐

Fuzzy Logic

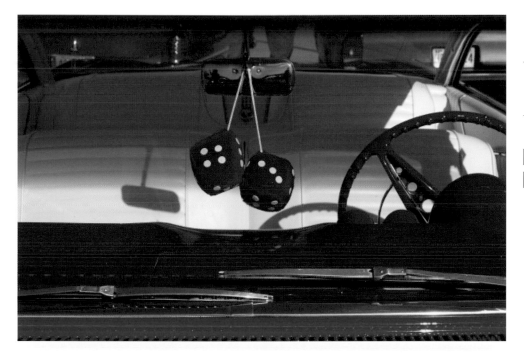

10 differences

Answers on page 133

Keep score:

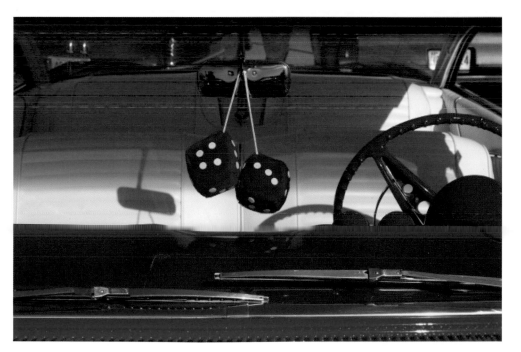

Every Which Way

Answers
on page 133

Keep score:

Taxing Taxiing

Whatever Floats Your Boat

Can you unscramble these three photos?

Answer on page 134

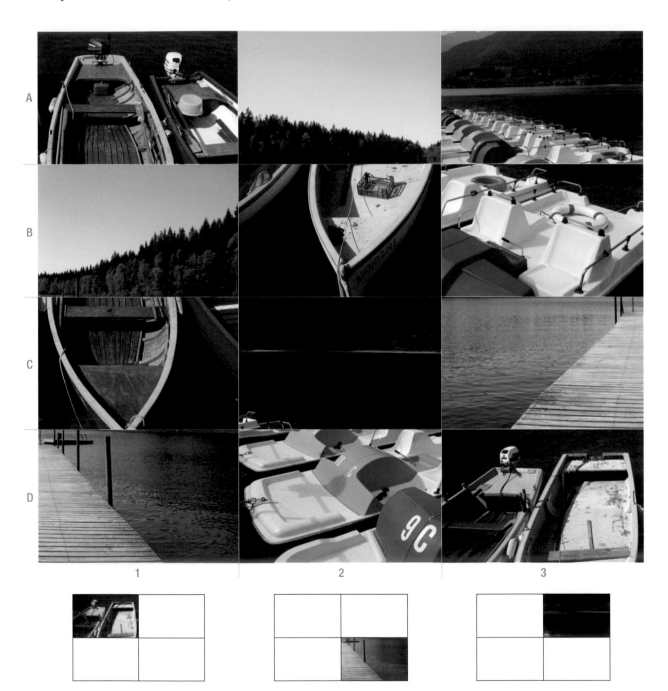

What's Moo With You?

Can you unscramble these three photos?

Answer on page 134

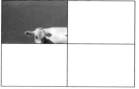

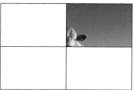

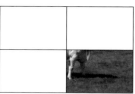

Two-Lane Teaser

Dog Tired

8
differences

Answers
on page 134

Keep score:

Too Many Tulips

EASY

10
differences

Answers
on page 135

Keep score:

☐ ☐ ☐ ☐ ☐
☐ ☐ ☐ ☐ ☐

The Great Wall

The Crate Wall

Cottage Industry

Liner Notes

Polly Gone

Can you find the ten parrots hidden in the photo below?

Answer on page 135

Suited to a Tee

Can you find the six golf balls hidden in the photo below?

Answer on page 136

Board Meeting

Feeling Feline

Can you locate the small images below in the large picture?

Answer on page 136

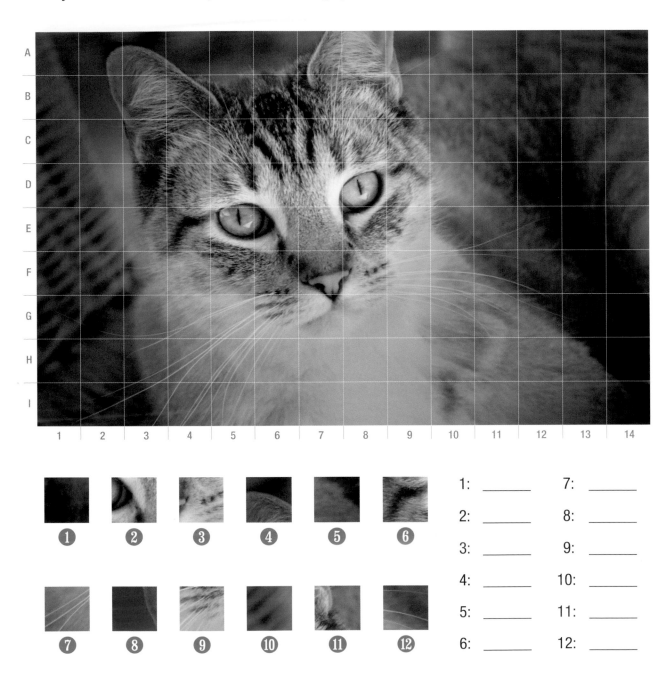

1: _____   7: _____

2: _____   8: _____

3: _____   9: _____

4: _____   10: _____

5: _____   11: _____

6: _____   12: _____

I Want to Be Leaves

Can you locate the small images below in the large picture?

Answer on page 136

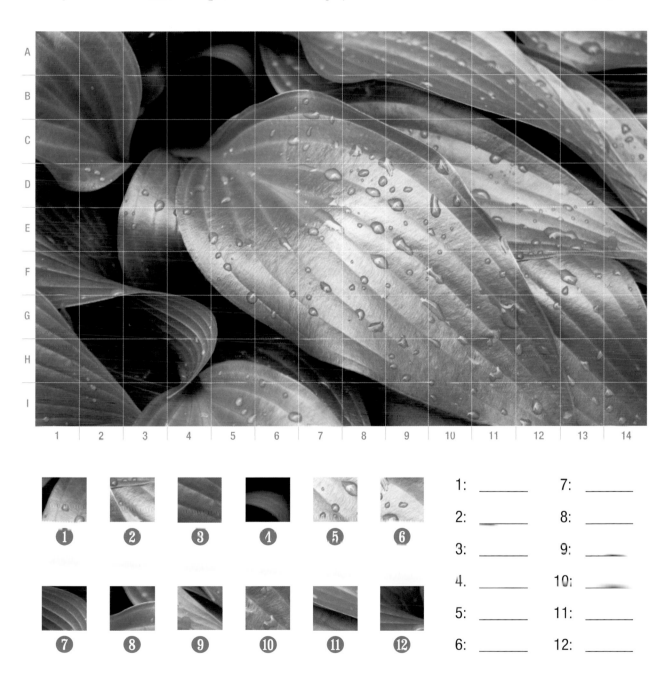

1: _____	7: _____
2: _____	8: _____
3: _____	9: _____
4: _____	10: _____
5: _____	11: _____
6: _____	12: _____

55

Mi Casa Es Su Conundrum

See Sawmill

Station Identification

Pedal Pushers

12
differences

Answers
on page 137

Keep score:

Wingside Seat

10 differences

Answers on page 137

Keep score:

A Pain in the Nectar

Which two of these photos are exactly alike?

Answer on page 137

Swing Fever

Which two of these photos are exactly alike?

Answer on page 137

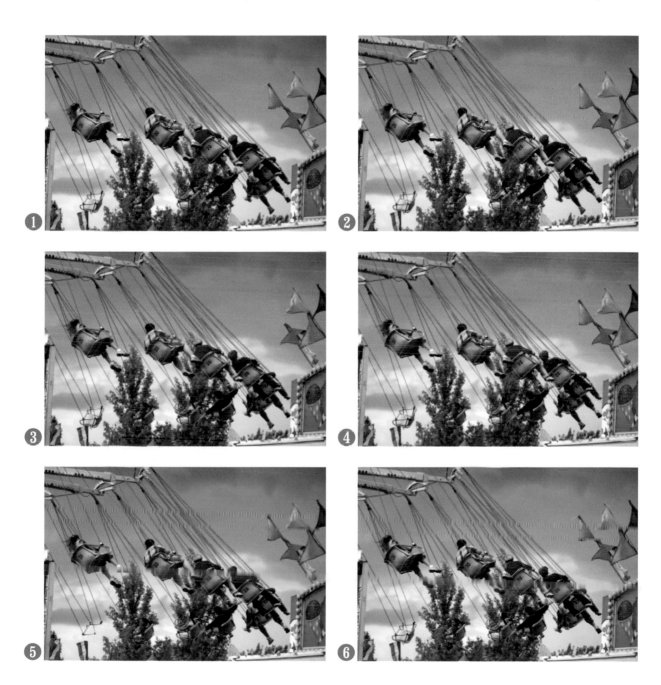

Berry Confusing

Can you unscramble these three photos?

Answer on page 137

Green Daze

Can you unscramble these three photos?

Answer on page 138

1   2   3

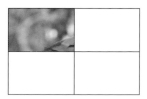
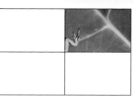

Up in the Air

Tower of Power

Formal Gathering

Dude, Where's My Car?

16
differences

Answers
on page 138

Keep score:

Just Deserts

Windows Update

HARD

12
differences

Answers
on page 139

Keep score:
☐ ☐ ☐ ☐ ☐
☐ ☐ ☐ ☐
☐ ☐

Circuit Circus

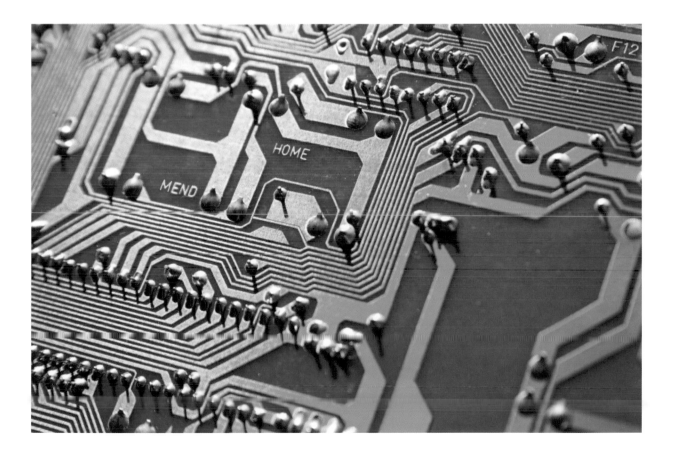

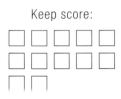

Slippery Helm

HARD

14
differences

Answers
on page 139

Keep score:

☐ ☐ ☐ ☐ ☐
☐ ☐ ☐ ☐
☐ ☐ ☐

Taking the Plunge

Which two of these photos are exactly alike?

Answer on page 139

Made in the Shade

Which two of these photos are exactly alike?

Answer on page 139

Bucolic Befuddlement

Train Strain

Plant Life

Can you unscramble these three photos?

Answers on page 140

City Life

Can you unscramble these three photos?

Answers on page 140

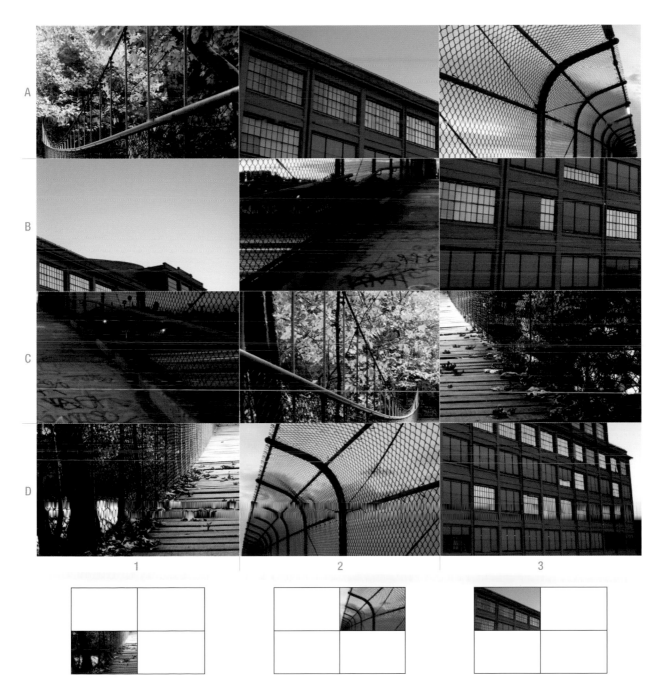

I Get a Kick Out of Euros

Overpass Overload

Shipshape

A Shining Example

Monkey Business

Which two of these photos are exactly alike?

Answer on page 141

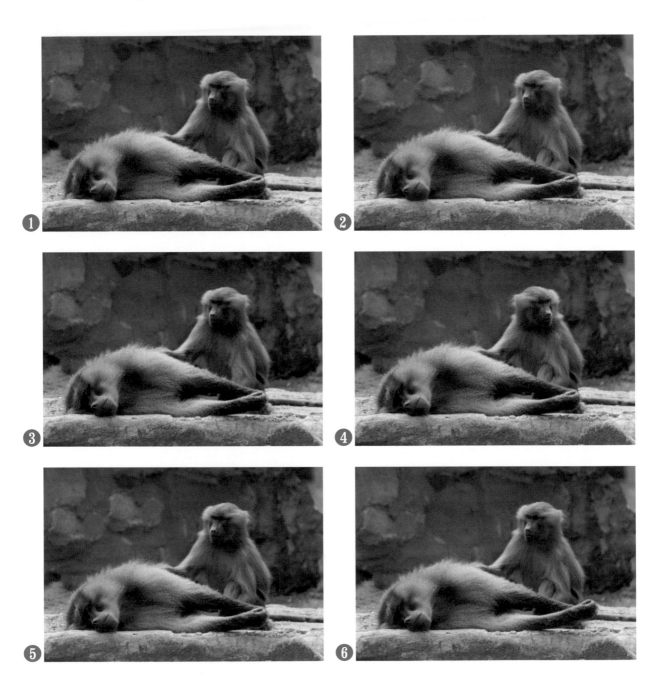

Hello, Dolls

Which two of these photos are exactly alike?

Answer on page 141

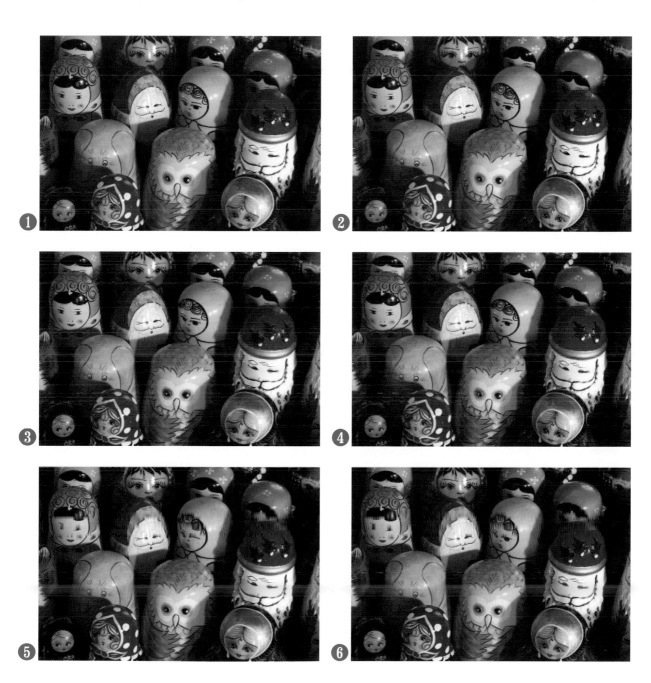

Happy Scamper

HARD

8
differences

Answers
on page 142

Keep score:

☐ ☐ ☐ ☐ ☐
☐ ☐ ☐

Tree-mendous

Can you locate the small images below in the large picture? Some may be rotated.

Answer on page 142

1: _____   7: _____

2: _____   8: _____

3: _____   9: _____

4: _____   10: _____

5: _____   11: _____

6: _____   12: _____

Cloud Crowd

Can you locate the small images below in the large picture? Some may be rotated.

Answer on page 142

1: _____   7: _____

2: _____   8: _____

3: _____   9: _____

4: _____   10: _____

5: _____   11: _____

6: _____   12: _____

Cathedral Confusion

10
differences

Answers
on page 142

Keep score:

Walkways This Way

Answers
on page 142

Keep score:

Going in Circles

Tall Disorder

Beach Buggy

Boat Sides Now

Crazy Daisies

Can you locate the small images below in the large picture? Some may be rotated.   Answers on page 143

	1: _____	7: _____
	2: _____	8: _____
	3: _____	9: _____
	4: _____	10: _____
	5: _____	11: _____
	6: _____	12: _____

Tarnation, Carnations!

Can you locate the small images below in the large picture? Some may be rotated.   Answers on page 143

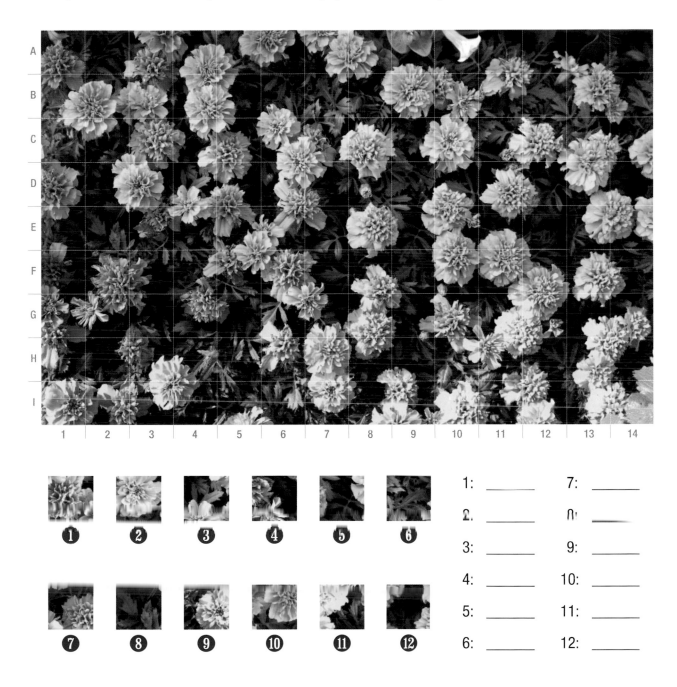

Mexican Mix-up

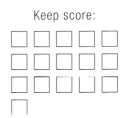

Flummoxing Fluttering

Which two of these photos are exactly alike?

Answer on page 143

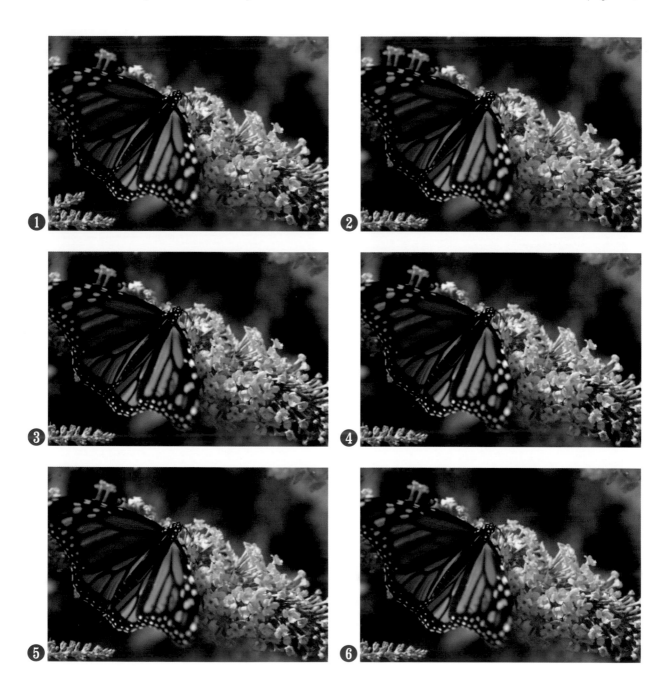

Baffling Bicycling

Which two of these photos are exactly alike?

Answer on page 143

❶ ❷

❸ ❹

❺ ❻

On the Waterfront

Bridge Out

Keep score:

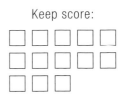

Gazebo Gazing

ANSWERS

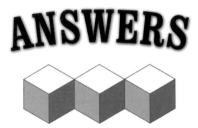

Fair Play

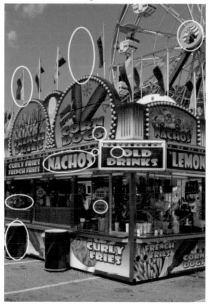

Hut One! Hut Two!

What's Up, Dock?

Hello, Yellow

1:	B13	5:	D4	9:	H3
2:	G4	6:	F2	10:	B5
3:	D8	7:	F13	11:	E10
4:	A12	8:	A2	12:	B10

Hi, Hyacinth

1:	B10	5:	A1	9:	A12
2:	E13	6:	F11	10:	F2
3:	G4	7:	H1	11:	E10
4:	B6	8:	D9	12:	B13

Vine and Dandy

Columns As You See 'Em

A Horse, of Course

Home on the Orange

Orange on the Home

Tennis, Anywhere?

Bumper Stumper

Making a Splash

Images 1 and 4 are alike.

132

Taking a Leap

Images 3 and 6 are alike.

Tunnel Vision

Texas Two-Step

Fuzzy Logic

Every Which Way

Taxing Taxiing

Whatever Floats Your Boat

D3	A1
B2	C1

A2	B1
C3	D1

A3	C2
D2	B3

What's Moo With You?

D3	B2
C1	A1

A2	C2
B1	C3

B3	D2
A3	D1

Two-Lane Teaser

Dog Tired

Too Many Tulips

The Great Wall

The Crate Wall

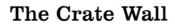

Cottage Industry

Liner Notes

Polly Gone

Suited to a Tee

Board Meeting

Feeling Feline

1:	D13	5:	H13	9:	G6
2:	E6	6:	E4	10:	E2
3:	F8	7:	H4	11:	B9
4:	A3	8:	B2	12:	F11

Mi Casa Es Su Conundrum

I Want to Be Leaves

1:	D3	5:	F8	9:	E14
2:	F12	6:	D9	10:	H11
3:	H1	7:	G4	11:	B10
4:	A5	8:	B6	12:	F2

See Sawmill

Station Identification

Pedal Pushers

Wingside Seat

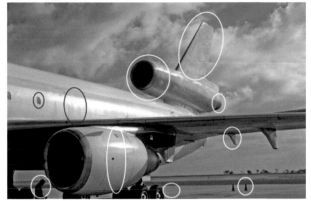

A Pain in the Nectar

Images 4 and 5 are alike.

Swing Fever

Images 2 and 4 are alike.

Berry Confusing

C1	A2
B3	D2

A1	B2
C3	D1

C2	A3
B1	D3

Green Daze

A3	B1
C2	D3

C1	A2
B3	D2

C3	A1
B2	D1

Up in the Air

Tower of Power

Formal Gathering

Dude, Where's My Car?

Just Deserts

Windows Update

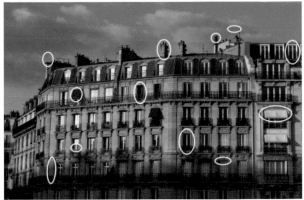

Circuit Circus

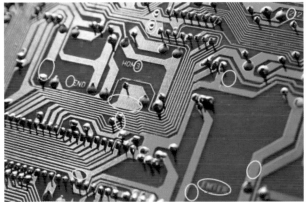

Slippery Helm

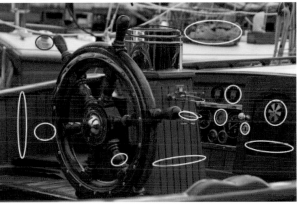

Taking the Plunge

Images 2 and 3 are alike.

Made in the Shade

Images 1 and 3 are alike.

Bucolic Befuddlement

Train Strain

Plant Life

A2	C1
B3	D3

A3	D1
B1	C2

D2	B2
A1	C3

City Life

C2	A1
D1	C3

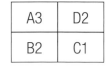

A3	D2
B2	C1

A2	B1
B3	D3

I Get a Kick Out of Euros

Overpass Overload

Shipshape

A Shining Example

Monkey Business

Images 2 and 5 are alike.

Hello, Dolls

Images 2 and 6 are alike.

141

Happy Scamper

Tree-Mendous

1:	D11	5:	G11	9:	H1
2:	I14	6:	C8	10:	I9
3:	E6	7:	F8	11:	E2
4:	A13	8:	A8	12:	A2

Cloud Crowd

1:	B5	5:	A10	9:	I3
2:	D2	6:	D7	10:	D10
3:	H10	7:	H2	11:	G4
4:	H8	8:	A8	12:	H12

Cathedral Confusion

Walkways This Way

Going in Circles

Tall Disorder

Beach Buggy

Boat Sides Now

Crazy Daisies

1:	E8	5:	C7	9:	F10
2:	F2	6:	F14	10:	G11
3:	B2	7:	C14	11:	C10
4:	H6	8:	I2	12:	G8

Mexican Mix-up

Tarnation, Carnations!

1:	F6	5:	E9	9:	I7
2:	C10	6:	B7	10:	B2
3:	D4	7:	C5	11:	G11
4:	G2	8:	E2	12:	D14

Flummoxing Fluttering

Images 4 and 5 are alike.

Baffling Bicycling

Images 1 and 6 are alike.

On the Waterfront

Bridge Out

Gazebo Gazing